Copyright © 2007, 2016 LaVerne Jackson-Harvey

All rights reserved. No parts of this book may be reproduced in any form or used without the permission from the author.
Second Edition

She can be reached at laverne.harvey@yahoo.com or visit her website at www.lavernejharvey.com if you would like to purchase additional copies of this book.

ISBN-10: 0-9909119-1-8
ISBN-13: 978-0-9909119-1-3

Life Circumstances: Do Not Let Life Circumstances Limit Your Outcome

It is my pleasure to share with you my Second Edition of poems called *Life Circumstances: Do Not Let Life Circumstances Limit Your Outcome*. It provides you an insight to many situations in life that we all experience such as pain, anger, parenting, fears, inspirations, and motivation.

We all have a poet in us. It comes out at different times in our lives. Many times, life circumstances dictate what we want to write about. The poem *Pain* was a cathartic piece for me. It allowed me to release some pent-up emotions of pain that I internalized after the passing of my mother, Lillie Ruth Jackson, many years ago. After I wrote this poem my creative juices awakened and these poems and many more that will be in my book *A Ray of Hope: Poems of Inspirations* started to flow. I have written over 100 poems that highlight life circumstances, life experiences, my commitment to children, and my culture. I have authored a children's book entitled **Ruth and Her Hoots**. I am sharing a couple of poems written by my son, Gary Harvey, when he was fourteen years old. I constantly tell him that he is my muse, my inspiration for many of my poems, especially those that talk about the plight of our black boys, such as **Mama's Boy and Don't Break their Spirit**.

Enjoy reading **Life Circumstances: Don't Let Life Circumstances Limit Your Outcome**. Many of these poems will make you think about your own life, reflect on what's going on with our children, and what we can do to make this a better world to live in. I would like to thank my family, friends, and colleagues for their support. Enjoy and find the inner poet in you.

Table of Contents

COUNT YOUR BLESSINGS 6
IT'S ALL ABOUT THE CHILDREN 8
THE SKY IS THE LIMIT 10
FIND YOUR WINGS 11
EDUCATE NOT INCARCERATE 12
ALL LIVES MATTER...BUT IT'S NOT EQUAL .. 16
PAIN 18
AN ODE TO PARENTS 20
THE MASK 25
BLACK CHILD 26
FACE YOUR FEARS 28
A RAY OF HOPE 30
BLACK GIRLS LIFT YOUR HEAD HIGH 32
HOPE 33
PROUD BLACK WOMAN 34
FRIENDS TO THE END 36
DO NOT LET LIFE'S CIRCUMSTANCES LIMIT YOUR OUTCOME 38
MOM, WE LOVE YOU 40
A LETTER TO MY FATHER 42
A JEWEL 44
MOVING UPWARD 47
YOUNG PEOPLE WAKE UP 48
FIGHT EVERYDAY WE MUST 49
BLACK EXCELLENCE 50

THE HISTORICAL PLIGHT OF THE STRONG
BLACK MAN 52
INTO THE NIGHT 56
SOCIAL BUTTERFLY 57
RISE 58
I'VE GOT THINGS TO DO 59
BELIEVE IN YOURSELF 60
THE GRADUATE 62
CLAFLIN UNIVERSITY-YOU ARE ONE OF A
KIND 63
THE ALPHA WOMEN 66
EBONY THOUGHTS AND QUOTES 69
ABOUT THE AUTHOR 73

Count Your Blessings

We all have blessings that are a part of our lives
The ability to wake up and see another day
The ability to see the beauty of God's work
To hear sounds of our environment and nature
To speak words of encouragement and
communicate with others
The joy of being with our family and friends
Food to nourish our bodies and share with our loved
ones
A lifetime partner to share our love
A roof over our heads for shelter and comfort
The opportunity to give back to our community
The thrill of meeting a goal we've set for ourselves
The ability to see the light during our darkest hour
and
Hope for a better day and peace around the world

The willingness to choose hope over hate during
tumultuous times in our country
The ability to dream the possible
The capacity to love unconditionally
The aptitude to learn
The fortitude to provide guidance, values, and
support for our children
The optimism to believe in the possibilities and not
be afraid of challenges
The strength to not let fear rule our actions and stop
us from living
But face our fears

With zest and zeal for life

This time of year, touches our hearts in so many
ways
It allows us to enjoy the moment and reflect on the
past
It allows us to smile as we think of our loved ones
no longer with us
We have so much in which to be thankful
Life, love, happiness, health, friends, family,
accomplishments, compassion for others, and God
in our lives

Share your gifts to impact on the life of someone in
need of hope
Who may be in pain, feel hopeless, alone, alienated,
and not worthy
Use your compassion to make a difference in the
lives of others
Keep your faith, embrace, and share your bounty
Be thankful for your life's circumstances and
Count your blessings

It's All About The Children

We must not forget that we were once children
Bright eyes, inquisitive, talkative, hyperactive, and questioning everything
We had dreams and aspirations
We played bear, hopscotch, red-light, marbles, mud bakery, caught june bugs, and fireflies
Our imagination was endless
We were allowed to be kids
Not trying to be adults before our time
We are now adults that had these experiences that make us who we are today

It's all about the children
Kids today have so many strikes against them
Many grow up way before their time
They want to be adults and are exposed to adult situations
Many skipped being a child because of their realities

It is all about the children
Who are not allowed to use their imagination
Many have no guidance
And behave in deplorable ways
They don't value your life or their own
Many are misdirected and have questionable values

We must save our children
We must believe in our children
Allowing them the opportunity to
Grow into productive and loving adults
We must all do our part to save our children
Because when it's all said and done
It's all about the children
Our future

The Sky is the limit
By
Gary Harvey
(Mama's Boy)

The sky is the limit
Follow your dream
No matter how hard
It may seem

Ignite your thoughts
Your sparks will inspire
Follow your ideas
Turn your dreams into a Fire

Rise over the mountain
What will you see?
A cloud, your dreams
High as can be

Discouragement is a hole
Don't fall in it
Always remember
The sky is the limit

Find Your Wings

Sometimes in life we feel we are falling and Unable
to fly
Because life happens
And we feel broken

This is the time we must test our faith
Reach for hope to keep us stable
Trust God because he has a plan for us
We may not know what it is
But God will show us the way

We may struggle to hold on
Trying not to fall
Looking for balance in our life

As time goes on we become stronger
Not letting fear of failure or disappointment stop us
We look back at those experiences and lessons that
were learned

Through these trying times
We find our way and
Are now ready to soar

We find our wings and fly
To our next adventure
We know that with God's guidance
We will survive

Educate Not Incarcerate

Education is
A means to an end
Our way out

We must know from whence we come
To know where we are going

Appreciate the past
Painful as it is
Sacrifice, blood, sweat, and tears
Strong, determined, relentless
Spirits soars through it all

As a people, we must stand tall
In spite of it all
Our stock is high
For education, many of our ancestors have died

Our contribution is plentiful
But to some our history is meaningless

Brothers and sisters
Wake up, we cannot sleep anymore
For many doors that were opened, many have closed

No longer be a prisoner of fear

Plot your path and go liberate your
Mind, body, and soul

We must be bold
Do not let others plot your destination

We are the captain of our ship
The more we know the further we will go
Knowledge is power

Education is the key
Unlock your cell full of anger, hopelessness,
distrust, fear, jealousy
Do not feel incarcerated

Use the key of education and make a difference
Lift yourself up and your brothers and sisters
Together we are no longer prisoners
But free to change, to uplift, to grow, to challenge,
to learn, to educate

We must educate our people
Not to be incarcerated by ignorance
We are our own gatekeepers….

Mama's Boy

Tall, dark and handsome
Son, a mother's dream
Busy, inquisitive, outgoing, shy, funny, smart
Development of brilliance
Mother's pray for them as they grow
Up against the odds
Teach survival skills, a way of life

Birth
A moment of joy and sadness
Joy for the wonderful boy who will become a great
Man, son, father, grandfather, role model
Sadness because of society's images and history's
Lessons about the black male, misunderstood,
Labeled, abused, stereotyped, genocide
Negative images in abundance

Mama's boy
Make you laugh, cry and proud
Laugh at their stories as they go through the various
Phases of manhood
Cry when you see their pain and you can't take it
Away…a part of the growing process
Proud to be his mama
Proud to see him grow from mama's boy to a
Strong, intelligent, kind, gentle, supportive,

Responsible, spiritual and resilient man of
Substance
Proud to see him be a husband, father, a rock for his
Children ...A Mama's Man

All Lives Matter…But It's Not Equal

All lives matter, but history has shown
That treatment of lives from different cultures is not equal
From our past to the future
Black lives have always been regarded with less value
We were not seen as full human beings
But counted as 3/5 of a person in our history

Our men were hung and treated less than a dog
Our women were raped without total regard to their feelings
Our children were taken from their parents and sold to the highest bidder
The family unit held on by a string

Black lives had to endure the Jim Crow Laws
Our ancestors were killed trying to get an education and making a better life for their children
They were forced to work from sunrise to sunset at the demand of their slave owners
This included men, women, and children

Through our strong foundation, our religion
And our determination to not let our spirits be broken
But continue to fight against injustices
We Are Still Standing

Our Black men were killed for anything including, looking at a white woman
They were found guilty of crimes without evidence
They were guilty until proven innocent, instead of innocent until proven guilty
Our strong Black men fought for their freedom despite threats against their lives
They fought to be with and provide for their wives and children
And to keep their families intact
They were feared by their slave owners because they would not go down without a struggle

When we say, all lives matter we must look at the Good, Bad, and Ugly of our history
We have to look at slavery, white privilege, discrimination, inequality, the dual system of justice, KKK, hate groups, racism, voting right suppression, unnecessary force and killing of our Black men at the hand of law enforcement officers, health care, crime, unequal educational opportunities, unemployment, gun rights, equal pay, politics, laws, disrespect of our first Black President, unequal coverage by the news media, oppression, lynching, and poverty, to name a few, to see where injustice exists

We once again must fight for justice caused by the injustices that exist
Let it be known that "Black Lives Do Matter"

Pain

Pain
Sharp
Deep
To the core
Bottled up but cannot open
Deeper, inside and out
The emotion is closed
It's hard to expose
Turning, churning, oozing as it implodes
Out with a sigh
Hurtful no lie
Ease, relief, slowly opening up from inside
Pain no more

DA BRAT

Daddies
Angel
Beautiful Daughter
Resilient
Alluring
Tenacious

Daddies dream of daughters like you
Playful, seeking guidance, fills their heart with joy
They dream of the young lady you will become
The choices you will make in life

They fear the unknown for their loved ones
Holding on as long as possible
Trying to keep you close knowing that one day they must let you go
They must let you grow into an independent, self-sufficient woman that is capable of taking care of herself and not have to depend on a man to survive

They know you will become part of someone else's life
DA BRAT that will become a wife, mother, grandmother, a rock for the family, a best friend
A loving daughter that will always be DA BRAT

An Ode to Parents

God created parents to bear and mold his children
This is one of the most awesome jobs on earth
However, many of us wonder if we are doing it right
There are no books that say if you do this your child will come out perfect
Because there are no perfect children

Our role as parents requires love, guidance, hardnosed tactics, tough love, unconditional love
We are our children's first teacher, caregiver, coach, friend, disciplinarian, and role model
This is a job that is 24/7
There are no breaks
Even when your child is not at home you have your child on your mind and in your heart
The payoff is that your children will grow up to be healthy, caring, productive, loving, conscionable, independent and outstanding citizens

You are not taught how to be a parent
You don't go to school and learn about the known and unknown responsibilities
The theories and practical strategies
You learn by trial and error
And many times there are many errors as they learn things such as burping, toilet Training,

breastfeeding, teething, breaking them from the bottle and pacifier, shopping, and multitasking many of their needs at once

They make you laugh and proud when they stand, crawl, take their first baby steps, mumble their first words mama and dada, walk and then run all over the place, and test your last nerves and stamina through the terrible twos as their inquisitive nature take hold and they have to touch and experience everything
They bring so much joy
And so much work
But they also make you question yourself a lot

Am I doing the right thing?
Is this how it is supposed to be done?
Is this too much medicine?
How do I open this stroller?
When do I feed them regular food?
Am I giving them too much?
Is their temperature too high?
How do I potty train?
Do they hear me?
How do I select a doctor for my child?
How do I select a dentist and is it too early?
Am I calling them too much?
What are they doing?
How did they learn that?
Are they teething or colicky?
Where are my keys?

When do I take them off the breast and bottle?
Am I crazy?
The list goes on and on...

Then it's time to go to a babysitter or daycare for those parents not able to stay at home with them.
You have fear and trepidation about this
Will my child be safe and nurtured?
Is the facility clean?
Will they change them on a regular basis?
How much does it cost?
What are they teaching my child?
Are they playing with other kids?
If they are sick will they call me?
If my child is crying will they hold and comfort them...
Questions, Questions, and more questions

At the same time you are also taking care of your needs and taking quick time outs so you have the energy to take on many of the prerequisites and roles; patience, clown, weightlifter, doctor mom and dad, track star, detective, taxi driver, cheerleader, worrier, wrestler, juggler, psychologist, planner, nurturer, you get the picture
Realizing your children's needs come first
As a parent, you make many sacrifices
And play many roles at once
Trying to do what's best for your child

Then they get ready to go to school
What school should I send my child to?
Are they prepared?
How do I select the best place?
What should I be teaching them?
Can my child compete?
How can I get involved and help prepare them?
How far is it from the house?
How will they get to school?
Will I have to put them on a bus-a big fear?
How are they cared for on the bus?
It is a frightening time for the child and parent?
The child is reluctant in the beginning but then they can't wait to leave you?
And you as a parent began to experience a bit of separation anxiety and realizing your child now have friends that rates as high on their list as you...
What about me!!!

Now a new chapter in their lives begins
It is also a new chapter for you as well
They have homework which means you have homework too
You have after school programs and weekend events
And you ask yourself when is too many or too few activities

You also experience your child making new friends or that they are having a hard time meeting other

kids and you try to figure out what is the problem and what can you do to help them adjust
Many times, they need you more than ever
They want you to play with them, read to them or hear them read to you, take them to the movies, sports events, talk to them, and love them
They need you to help them through this period as they find out new things about themselves and other people.

The Mask

The face shows
What you want to see
But is that person
Really me
The smile, the look, the joy, the sound
Deep down inside it's really a frown
You see what you want to see
The mask shows a part of me
Look deeper and you will see
Who's really inside
The real me

Black Child

Black child
The fruit of a rich vine
Grounded deep in history
Has a unique story to tell

Full of substance
Resilient and strong
Strive in spite of shackles
Strong in the face of being denied
The same opportunities to flourish
Nourished with the blood of their ancestors

Black child
Full of life and dreams
Excel in spite of struggles and challenges
Rooted in a strong people
A strong history

Black child
Loved unconditionally by their family
Guided by life's lessons, God, and the belief
That they too are worthy, brilliant, and they can make a difference

Black child
Who will be the vine, the root and the substance
For their family

Guiding future black children to not believe all the negative images about them
And how to be a leader and overcome adversity

Black child
You are the light
Shining bright
Making inroads for the future
Leading you to grow, face challenges, make good decisions, and be a unique individual
Continuing to strengthen your past, present, and future

Face Your Fears

An emotion that stops you in your tracks
Causing you to feel tense
Paralyzing
Heart beat fast
Pulse increasing
Anxiety high
Makes you afraid to take risks
Sometimes stifling your growth
For fear of failure or consequences
You avoid the unknown
Staying in the dark
Afraid of the outcome
Sometimes you live with the unknown
For fear of the known

Fear can challenge your desire to live
Frightening you to the point you don't want to go anywhere
It can lead to phobias

As difficult as it is to face your demons
You must not let it stop you from living
Take the steps to face your fears
Live your life to the fullest
Challenging yourself to move, not freeze, in time
Take steps to live your life
Face your fears

"DO NOT LET OTHERS DIM
YOUR LIGHT
LET IT SHINE BRIGHT
BECAUSE
THERE IS ALWAYS THAT RAY
OF HOPE"

A Ray of Hope

Let not life's circumstances dim your light
Of
What could and can be
Believe
That you deserve all that's offered if you put out
equal effort
Continue to believe in your potential
Never question your capability
Strive for excellence
Believe in yourself
Believe in your future
Believe in who you want to be
Do not let others dim your light
Let it shine bright
Because
There is always that ray of hope

"BLACK GIRLS-EMBRACE YOUR BODY, NOSE, LIPS, HIPS, EYES, SIZE, HAIR AND SHADES OF EBONY, LOVE THE SKIN YOU ARE IN"

Black Girls Lift Your Head High

Black girls lift your head high
Above the negative images displayed about you

The offensive words used to describe you
The stereotypes that those in power choose to
continue to use to put you down

You are above that
You are a survivor and strive
In spite of efforts to keep you down, lower your
self-esteem, and devalue your beauty
Embrace your body, nose, lips, hips, eyes, size, hair,
and shades of ebony
Love the skin you are in

Black girls lift your head high
You are here for a purpose
Embrace your uniqueness
Love yourself, respect your body, and demand
respect
Embrace your gifts, your history, and your future

Black girls lift your head high
Knowing that God makes no mistakes
And he made you

Hope

Hope allows us to see
The future where possibilities exist
Hope helps us to forget the
Pain of the past and know life can be better
Hope allows us to heal
And see the joy
Hope helps us to believe in ourselves and others
Hope let us know that through
Trials and tribulations there is a better way
Hope allows us to see the best in ourselves
And forgive mistakes we've made in the past
Hope helps us to get up in the morning
And face a new day
Hope lifts us up when we fall
Not allowing us to stay down
It challenges us to think
Beyond the moment
Hope allows us to see
During our darkest hours
Hope will lift you high and
Not allow you to fall into the abyss
A ray of hope shines bright, is electrifying,
Shocking us to new heights and will not allow us to
Fall into harms way
But through God see a better way

Proud Black Woman

Beautiful
Shades and shapes undeniable
Lips full and luscious
Striking curves
That accentuates the body
Features created to show the beauty of the Black
Woman

Hair
Natural, curly, straight
Beautiful coarseness that's unique and
Show's personality

Women of character, grace and poise
Dignified in times of oppression
Strong in times of rejection, abuse, and injustices

History has not been kind to this strong black
woman
Who has been subjected to rape
Children taken and sold
Men and husbands dehumanized
Separated from her family
Abused, degraded, and many times made to feel less
than human
Like an object without feelings

Through her faith, will, and desire to be who God made her to be
She takes her gifts to provide for her family
Love and support her man
And raise her children to become loving and caring human beings

The proud black woman
In spite of all she has endured
She has survived
To rise beyond the negatives
Acknowledging her past
Becoming stronger because of the sacrifices of black women before her
Looking to the future with faith, anticipation, and hope

Friends To The End

They know the good, bad, and ugly and still love you unconditionally

Friends are good listeners
They hear you when you go on, and on, and on
Sometimes about things that are important
Sometimes to let you vent

Friends will cry with you when you are sad and in times of need
They do not see you as weak because you are expressing your feelings

Friends bring out the best in you
They relish in your accomplishments
Proud to see you meet your goals
Proud to see you be successful

Friends will tell you the truth
To help you avoid making a mistake
They are not brutal, but honest
So you can see yourself through other lenses

Friends don't always see eye to eye
But they don't hold your opinion against you

Friends don't try to change you to be who they want you to be
They accept you for who you are

Friends love the time they share together, having fun, laughing, plotting,
And rejuvenating to face the world

Friends are there through life events, marriage, children, college, and death
They are an integral part of life

Friends are few and beyond
Not all acquaintances deserve the title

Friends are genuine, honest, trustworthy, a clown, a rock, a thinker, a lover

Friends can be one mile or thousand miles away
And they still touch your heart, touch your lives, and are a part of your being

Friends are there through thick and thin
They are with you until the end, friendship is forever

Do Not Let Life's Circumstances Limit Your Outcome

Some people are blessed with material riches, opportunities for success are a part of life's expectations. They are privileged to have their basic needs met...employment, health care, education, food, and housing. They go to the best schools, take the most rigorous college preparation classes, they are taught by highly qualified teachers who have high expectations for them and they attend summer camps or precollege programs. Their future is set and it's up to them to take what is given to them and make their future better.

Other's are products of poverty, food is not promised, a roof over there heads is not guaranteed, unemployment, single family household, live paycheck to paycheck, disappointments, and failure are a part of life, no medical services are available, and violence is a part of their daily being.

Their children attend schools where some teachers don't believe in them, they have low expectations for the children, many are not highly qualified, and work for a paycheck-not the dividend of making a positive difference in the life of a child. Children are told to take high school classes that will not prepare them for college but for minimum wage jobs, and they do not attend summer camps and Pre-college programs…the streets are their summer opportunities.

In spite of these circumstances, these children have what it takes to be successful. History has shown that many students who are products of families with less means have triumphed and been successful in spite of life's negative curve and many with the means and the foundation have failed in spite of having the best of everything.

We must teach all our children that despite life circumstances, positive outcomes are available to them.

MOM, We Love You

Everyone has a mom but many share the void of
Not having that special person present but existing
in their heart

They love and remember no less
The person who loved them unconditionally

The mom that would give you her last dollar
The mom that imparted her values, strength and
Sense of being the best you can be
The mom that even though she is gone to a higher
place
Continues to touch your heart in so many ways

Mom, you are missed more than you can ever
imagine
You are a very gracious southern woman
Who was concerned about others all the way to the
end
This is a characteristic that defines you

We miss your Mona Lisa smile,
Your words of advice,
Those special moments that only we know about
The love and guidance you imparted on your
children, grandchildren
And all the other extended siblings

We miss all there is about you
You may not be here in the flesh
But you are always close our hearts,
In our mind, in our being

We are so grateful that God gave us to you
And we know that you continue to be the
Mom of Moms in the great beyond

We will continue to cherish the package,
The gift and the content
You are the greatest gift of all
You are our MOM

A Letter To My Father

Dad, I dream about who you were
How you and mom met
The void in my life
You and mom brought eleven beautiful children
Into the world
Eight boys and three girls
And I was the last child
All your children's name start with L
The first letter of love
God took you from us at a very young age
And I was at the young age of 3 months
I cannot remember your presence, your touch, your
face, your smile and
Who you were

I know you were special because
You had a phenomenal wife
She reflected the both of you
Through her courage, strength, guidance, and
nurturing and value
I know life was not easy
Providing for your family was difficult
And I'm sure we were a handful
In your pictures I see glimpses
Of you in each of us
And that makes me smile
I remember Father's Day
That was difficult to me

Everyone else did special things
To recognize their dad
But I could not relate
I remember days in school when
We drew pictures of family and
I had no image of you to draw

As I grew older there was a level of pain and regrets
Regrets for not having you to take me to school
Regrets of not having a memory of you
Regrets of not seeing your smile
Regrets of not having you to spoil me
Regrets that we could not take a family picture
Regrets that you could not come to my wedding and
walk me down the aisle
Regrets that you did not meet my husband and your
grandchildren
Regrets for my loss
This however did not make me less of a person
We were rich in love
I know you are a part of me
You are in my soul and being
You helped to make me who I am
You may be gone but you not forgotten
You and mom can reignite your love in heaven
You are my father and
I will always love you

A Jewel

What is a jewel?
It is a precious stone that is lovely, brings joy,
shines and continues to appreciate in Value,
My jewel is Francis Starms Discovery Learning
Center,
It is a secret of so many successes

It has provided my child and others the opportunity
to learn in a safe and nurturing Environment where
expectations are set high and not compromised;
Teachers are trained to work with all children,
They receive continuous staff development and
Children are encouraged to strive for excellence
In a "Can Do" environment;

The support staff is key as well;
They know the children;
Encourage the children
They are a member of the village

It models the black college experience for our kids,
Instilling confidence
That in spite of life's circumstances
You will be successful
You can be what you want to be
And failing is not an option

Students are taught to be proud of their culture,
Be proud of their ancestors and know how their
contributions made it possible
For them to get an education today,
They are taught about the struggles,
accomplishments, inventions, leaders, their
Forefathers, slavery, sweat, blood, and grit of a
people achieving despite negative Treatment,
oppression, racism, and inequalities

They are taught they come from a strong people,
A proud people,
An accomplished people
With a strong history that will take them to places
they can only dream

They are encouraged to use their gifts
Be it drama, forensics, sports, dance, creative
writing, music and expressing who they are and
what they want to be

Our precious gems, Little Black Boys
Are not seen as troubled kids but as future leaders
Energy is channeled so learning can occur
Nurturing is a part of Starm's family mantra
Allowing these young men to feel safe and provide
opportunities for them to transition into adolescents
and manhood without fear that they can't be
themselves
Teaching them about character development and
responsibilities

Parents are valued as a part of the village
Participation is encouraged in the growth of their child
Parents are welcomed and invited to get involved
In all aspects of the school

Leadership is strong
A vision is clear and a plan is present
To ensure all kids are successful despite their circumstances

Starms I salute you for your
Vision, your beliefs in our children
The nurturing you provide
Your no nonsense but caring stance
And your high expectations and belief
That our children are valued, smart, funny, future leaders, and
They are 100% college material that will be productive and successful in meeting life's
Challenges.
You will continue to be a "JEWEL" that shines, is polished, and bring out the gifts of our Youth
Priceless....

Moving Upward

Moving in all directions
Wondering where to go
Where will you land
Never standing still

It's frightening to move
In unknown territories
Not knowing what's in store for you

You can choose to move
In the familiar
Where comfort exists
And is the norm

Or

You can choose to venture into the new
The unknown
Excited about the challenges
The thrills that lie ahead

Whichever direction you go
Just know that life is full of upward bounds
Into the future
Allow yourself to move up and explore
Knowing that your foundation
Will keep you strong

Young People Wake Up

Young people wake up
And take the challenge before you
You are our future
And that can be frightening
Not only to you
But to everyone
You have so much potential
There are no limitations to your future
But you
You can rise beyond the peer pressure,
unemployment, teenage pregnancies, gangs, drugs
And other ills that are out there
To steer you in the wrong direction
Making good choices is part of living
Wake up young people
Because the choices you make
Will impact on your future

Fight Everyday We Must

Black
Beautiful and blessed
Misunderstood and labeled
Why
Because of the color of our skin
Beautiful and brown, almond, black, and caramel
Shades undeniable
Black and proud
Yes, indeed
Rights denied
Opportunities denied
Fight everyday we must
Taught to feel inferior
Invisible history
Resilient people
Strong, determined, brilliant, passionate, survivors
Fight everyday we must
We wear the badge of color
Tan others seek to acquire
God's gift to us
Fight everyday we must
For our children, our ancestors, and ourselves

Black Excellence

Black Excellence defines us
In spite of injustices, racism, slavery, and
The attempt to dehumanize a race of people
We are still standing tall

Despite attempts in the past to not educate our ancestors
To threaten those who dared to make a difference
Despite shackles
We rose over the hill to see our future, to see the light,
To see freedom

As a people, we are strong, beautiful, Black, proud and achievers
We have made great contributions to this country,
To this society and all over the world

We must continue to stand tall
To strengthen others so they do not fall
Into the trap of not believing in themselves
Not loving themselves
Not embracing their God given gifts

We must propel them to dream
We must educate them on our magnificent history and

Our long list of accomplishments in all areas of academia
Black Excellence recognizes the brilliance, the grit, the growth, achievements, and
The strength of a strong, resilient, and proud people

The Historical Plight of the Strong Black Man

How do you describe the Strong Black Man?
He is all shades of ebony, handsome, and
Has intelligence in abundance

History has not been kind to our Black Men
Despite all the humiliation
Efforts of emasculation
Being treated worse than an animal
Devalued and hated
Our Black men are still standing

Many endured more pain
Then any human being should be allowed to feel
They were put in a position
Of enduring humiliation
As a survivor mechanism
They watched their women and daughters being raped
Children sold to the highest bidder
And themselves sold to the highest bidder
Because of their size not their minds
They were murdered because of the color of their skin
Not because they committed a crime

Our strong Black men
Worked hard in the fields

Threatened constantly for being rebellious
Many were killed for looking at a White woman
They walked with their head bowed because
If they looked in the eyes of a White person
They could die

When we look at slavery
We look at the injustices
Our people endured
But none as inhumane
As the treatment of Black men

Many lynching's occurred because the Black Man
Stood up for his rights, his family and his people
Many occurred because the White man had the
power to destroy a life, not having any guilt
Because they viewed him as nothing but a nigger
And they were the justice system

Hatred was paramount during this time
White children were taught to hate blacks
To see them as beneath them
That they were not to be respected
But they expected Black adults and children
To respect them because to their race
They were taught their race was superior
And provided them privileges, entitlements and
They emulated their parents

Black men were acknowledged for their athleticism
Humor, music, and dance

Not their intelligence
They were taught they were not smart,
Not handsome, self-hatred, not worthy of an education,
To be servants, to serve the White man, to be docile,
To endure humiliations
Not seen as a human being
Entitled to rights of dignity, protection, support their family, and all civil liberties

Our Black men were smart
They taught our Black boys how to survive
They taught them how to play the game
And fight for change
They taught them that Whites can
Abuse, humiliate and treat them disrespectful but
They can't take away your mind and soul
Our Black boys were taught
How to become Black men

We salute our warriors
Our protectors, our strong Black intelligent brothers
The development of this country was built on
The blood, sweat, and tears of our ancestors
Today many of the same injustices still applies
Our strong Black men
Still have to struggle
Endure a dual justice system
Live with the impact of past injustices
Not treated as equals and

Having to still prove themselves despite many achievements

They are loving husbands, fathers, grandfathers, brothers, and uncles
That are teaching their sons how to be a man
Black boys have three strikes against them at birth,
They are Black babies
They are Black boys and
They will be Black men
We must not allow their spirit to be broken
But teach them how to survive and become
Responsible, resilient, intelligent, spiritual
And strong Black men

Into the Night

into the night
dark
silent
oblivious to change
provides ambiance to nightlife
the backdrop for the moon to shine bright
it can be eerie and heighten one's fear
into the night
move with calm
awareness
eagerness
and
do not be blinded
by the great unknown

Social Butterfly

Social
Talkative
Peer group induced
Always having something to say
Something to do
Somewhere to go
On, and on, and on
Sometimes mistaken for disrespect
A troublemaker
Misunderstood
The social butterfly is an extrovert
People oriented
Channel the energy to group projects and use
cooperative learning
Develop leadership skills
The social butterfly
Is a beautiful and colorful creation ready to fly
And conquer the world

Rise

down
falling further in
trying to stand
weighted by demons
holding you still
not moving
slowly you make progress
floating to the top
rising above pain, hurt, bad judgement and demons
seeing the light

I've Got Things To Do
By
Gary Harvey
(Mama's Boy)

I've got things to do
Can't you let me be?
I know you care a lot
As I'm sure you can see

I've been working for hours
So on and so on
I need to relax my nerves
Please, please be gone

I have me a life
You gave it to me
But remember it's mine
Really

Now that I'm done
What will I do?
I need someone to talk to
How about you?

Believe In Yourself

Believe in yourself
You are worthy
You are capable
Believe in who you are, where you want to go
And know you will reach your goals
Do not let others define you
Limit your potential and
Break your spirit
Life is full of ups and downs
Highs and lows
It's up to you how you handle these difficult times
in your life
You can let self-doubt rule
And stay down, waddling in sorry
Or
You can let hope lift you high
Push you beyond belief and
Closer to your dreams
Knowing the process requires you to
Crawl, walk, and then run
With your head held high
A stride in your walk and
Confidence in who you are

Believe in yourself
Even when others don't
When you are told you can't reach your goal

Use this as a challenge to propel yourself into action
Because action speaks louder then words

Believe in yourself
Love yourself
Challenge yourself
The more you believe in yourself
The more you will achieve
Knowing that life is full of challenges, fears, and inhibitions,
Embrace your potentials
Embrace your gifts and
Believe that you will SUCCEED

The Graduate

Life is a journey
That has many twist and curves
Many times the road is rough
But we continue to travel our course
Because life can be bumpy
There are many turns
That led in different directions
You must ponder which way to go
As a graduate, you have traveled the right road
You have made choices that
Led to positive outcomes
You made it through high school, test, relationships
Roommates, peer pressure, trials and tribulations
and life decisions
And now you've reached this journey in your life-
GRADUATION
This has been a goal that was long term
But now the time is near
May you continue to make choices that will
Elevate you to new heights
Challenge you intellectually
And
Take you to your next adventure
May your future continue to be bright
We salute you-Our Graduate

Claflin University-You Are One Of A Kind

Claflin University
You are one of a kind
Touching the lives of many black students
Challenging them to succeed
Imparting knowledge, a since of purpose, cultural pride and confidence

You believed in us when others didn't
You did not see us as failures, deficient, incapable of learning
You saw the brilliance in us
You saw the potential
You ignited the spark

You taught us about our history
You taught us to love ourselves
We no longer had an invisible history
But a proud history
Our voices were heard, not silenced
And we lifted them higher

You touched me as a student
Many years ago
When I was going through the era of Jim Crow and segregation

I was fighting to be educated

Fighting to be heard
Fighting to belong
Fighting for my rights
My energy was slowly being depleted
But you gave me hope
You revived my soul and spirit

You allowed me to be a student
I didn't have to fight to belong
You embraced and guided me
You taught me about our ancestors who died for us
So that we could have a better life
And who made tremendous contributions to make this country great
You taught me to be a better person
And provided me the needed nurturing, guidance, and instruments of excellence

Through Claflin I felt like the burden of the world had been lifted off my shoulder
And I could breath and believe in myself and my future
I could be a student
Free to learn without distractions
You gave me a ray of hope that life can be good
You provided me with the tools I needed to get a terminal degree
You bestowed upon me the foundation to go anywhere and succeed

So, I say to you Claflin University
Thank you for believing in me
Thank you for the keys of education
Thank you for filling my mind with knowledge
And giving me the edge needed to compete
Thank you for seeing my potential
And preparing all your students to face the world
And step up to the challenge
You are one of a kind

The Alpha Women

Alpha represents the beginning
Alpha Kappa Alpha Sorority is the first Greek sorority providing guidance for other sororities that followed
The Alpha Woman represents women of character
She is strong, loving, nurturing and intelligent
The Alpha woman is dedicated to the causes of the sorority
The Alpha woman is a civil servant and she gives of herself to strengthen her family
And the community

The Alpha Woman is the rock of her family, community and are leaders
She wears many roles-wife, mother, grandmother, sister, auntie and friend
The Alpha Woman does not put any man before God, herself and her children
The Alpha Kappa Alpha woman strengthens the sorority through strong sisterhood
And a since of purpose

The Alpha Kappa Alpha woman wears the colors of pink and green to show pride
And showcase the beauty of Alpha
The Alpha Woman is a woman of character, grace and poise
Dignified in times of oppression

And strong in times of challenges, rejections, abuse and injustices
She imparts pearls of wisdom
Teaching sorors through her knowledge and experiences

The Alpha woman teaches her daughters that despite efforts to keep you down,
Lower your self-esteem and devalue your beauty
Love the skin you are in
She teachers her daughters to respect herself, her body and to strive to be a Woman of character and not to settle for less than a man of substance
She teaches her sons to respect women, how to become a man of substance and how to survive.

The sorority showed me the value of sisterhood, leadership and community service
It helped me to develop organizational skills and grow into a proud Black woman

The Alpha Kappa Alpha Sorority has shown longevity, fortitude and strength
By continuing to grow despite challenges and celebrating its Centennial –1908-2008…100 years of Alpha

The Alpha Kappa Alpha woman is confident, giving, leaders, organizers, planners, women of character, philanthropist, supporters, family oriented, community supporters, role models, educators, and mentors. They wear many roles to catapult the sorority and the next generation of sorors to future centennials.

Happy Birthday Alpha Kappa Alpha Sorority!!!

EBONY THOUGHTS AND QUOTES

"FIGHT EVERYDAY WE MUST
WE WEAR THE BADGE OF COLOR
TAN OTHERS SEEK TO ACQUIRE
GOD'S GIFT TO US"

"EDUCATION IS THE KEY
UNLOCK YOUR CELL FULL OF ANGER,
HOPELESSNESS, DISTRUST, FEAR,
JEALOUSY
DO NOT FEEL INCARCERATED
USE THE KEY OF EDUCATION
AND MAKE A DIFFERENCE"

"ANGER-RELEASE THOSE EMOTIONS TO
MAKE BETTER DECISIONS
STRENGTHEN YOURSELF AND REDIRECT
YOUR RAGE TO MAKE CHOICES
THAT WILL GUIDE YOUR FUTURE
NOT THE MOMENT"

"THEY NEED TEACHERS WILLING TO PUT
FORTH THE EXTRA EFFORT NEEDED TO
REACH AND TEACH THEIR STUDENTS
AND SAVE THEM FROM DROWNING"

'WOMEN OF CHARACTER TEACH THEIR DAUGHTERS TO RESPECT HERSELF, HER BODY, TO STRIVE TO BE A WOMAN OF CHARACTER, AND NOT SETTLE FOR LESS THAN A MAN OF SUBSTANCE"

"FRIENDS-THEY KNOW THE GOOD, BAD, AND UGLY AND STILL LOVE YOU UNCONDITIONALLY"

"PARENTING-THIS IS A JOB THAT IS 24/7 THERE ARE NO BREAKS"

"WAKE UP BLACK PEOPLE
WE MUST LEARN TO NOT BE OUR OWN WORST ENEMY, BUT BE OUR OWN SUPPORTERS
BECAUSE AT THE END OF THE DAY
WE ARE ALL WE'VE GOT"

"TIME-IT EPITOMIZES EQUAL OPPORTUNITY,
DOES NOT DISCRIMINATE"

"YOU AVOID THE UNKNOWN
STAYING IN THE DARK
AFRAID OF THE OUTCOME
SOMETIMES YOU LIVE WITH THE UNKNOWN
FOR FEAR OF THE KNOWN"

"DO NOT LET OTHERS DIM YOUR LIGHT
LET IT SHINE BRIGHT BECAUSE
THERE IS ALWAYS THAT RAY OF HOPE"

"BLACK GIRLS-EMBRACE YOUR BODY, NOSE, LIPS, HIPS, EYES, SIZE, HAIR AND SHADES OF EBONY, LOVE THE SKIN YOU ARE IN"

"SLOWLY YOUR VOICE IS HEARD
SILENCE TURNS TO SOUND"

"THERE ARE NO LIMITATIONS TO YOUR FUTURE BUT YOU"

"PAY IT FORWARD AND SHARE KINDNESS BECAUSE YOU DON'T KNOW WHOSE LIFE YOU MAY CHANGE"

"OUT OF SACRIFICES COMES RESULTS THAT CAN BRING JOY FOR A LIFETIME"

"WE MUST ALL DO OUR PART TO SAVE OUR CHILDREN"

"OUR LITTLE BLACK BOYS HAVE THREE STRIKES AGAINST THEM AT BIRTH, THEY ARE BLACK BABIES, THEY ARE BLACK BOYS, AND THEY WILL BE BLACK MEN...WE MUST NOT ALLOW THEIR SPIRIT TO BE BROKEN!"

"DAYDREAMING TAKES YOU PLACES THAT'S NEAR AND DEAR, PROVIDES TIME FOR INTROSPECTION"

"THE SOCIAL BUTTERFLY IS A BEAUTIFUL AND COLORFUL CREATION READY TO FLY AND CONQUER THE WORLD"

"RACE IS A DIVIDE IN THIS COUNTRY. WHEN THERE IS AN ISSUE THAT HAS A RACIAL OVERTONE, THERE IS USUALLY A RACIAL DIVIDE"

About the Author

Dr. LaVerne Jackson-Harvey has over thirty-five years of experience in K-12 and postsecondary education in counseling, advising, research, teaching, public speaking, and program design. She started writing her poetry at a late, but exciting time in her life. She has authored over 100 poems. She published two books of poetry entitled *Life Circumstances* and *A Ray of Hope*. She recently wrote a children's book entitled *Ruth and Her Hoots*. She received her Bachelors Degree from Claflin University, Masters Degree from Bowling Green State University, and Doctorate from Marquette University.

While employed at Marquette University, she founded The Night of Black Literature, a program that allowed students and staff to read their favorite poetry by African American authors. She has read her poetry at numerous events. She is the wife of Robert L. Harvey and the mother of three children, Dalila Granger, Rashida Harvey, and Gary Harvey. She was raised in Inman, South Carolina and lived in Milwaukee, Wisconsin. She currently resides in Charlotte, North Carolina.

www.ingramcontent.com/pod-product-compliance
Lightning Source LLC
Chambersburg PA
CBHW030913170426
43193CB00009BA/829